Muffin's
LOVE

Frank D'Erminio

CROSSBOOKS

CrossBooks™
A Division of LifeWay
1663 Liberty Drive
Bloomington, IN 47403
www.crossbooks.com
Phone: 1-866-879-0502

©2010 Frank D'Erminio. All rights reserved.

No part of this book may be reproduced, stored in a retrieval system, or transmitted by any means without the written permission of the author.

First published by CrossBooks 11/20/2010

ISBN: 978-1-6150-7642-0 (sc)

Library of Congress Control Number: 2010940879

Printed in the United States of America

This book is printed on acid-free paper.

Any people depicted in stock imagery provided by Thinkstock are models, and such images are being used for illustrative purposes only.

Certain stock imagery © Thinkstock.

Because of the dynamic nature of the Internet, any Web addresses or links contained in this book may have changed since publication and may no longer be valid. The views expressed in this work are solely those of the author and do not necessarily reflect the views of the publisher, and the publisher hereby disclaims any responsibility for them.

This book is dedicated to my mother and father
whose love for their children is like
God's love for all of us.

Muffin's Puppy Photo

Contents

Before Muffin Was Born. 1

My First Years with Muffin. .3

What Muffin Liked 9

A Long Goodbye 17

My Life as a Probation Officer 25

Being Humble 27

The Presence of God. 31

Pray Daily 33

Daily Growth. 35

The Face of Love 37

The Journey of Life. 39

Muffin Tells Her Story 43

The Gift. 47

Test of Faith 51

Before Muffin Was Born

In the deepest sleep that one could ever know came a soothing voice that said: "You are about to be born. Your only purpose in life is to love your master and all of his family forever. You will leave your mother, your father, your sisters and brothers. You might never see them again, but you are bound in the same purpose. A dog's life is to love and serve the master. You will eat, sleep, and play with your master. You will wait for him. You will listen to him. You will obey him. You will delight in him. Eventually, without realizing it, you will lay down your life for him. It is by these standards that your greatness will be measured." If only we could learn to love and serve our Master as well as Muffin loved and served hers.

Muffin's first thoughts were probably that she does not remember much about being with her family, except that on her birthday, February 10, 1995, she woke up and felt the wonderful warmth of her mom. Her brothers and sisters were always there. All were in a race to get to Mom, who was an endless supply of milk and love.

Mom was beautiful, and Muffin loved looking at her. She was white and fluffy and she loved her puppies. All

Muffin had to do was to eat and sleep all day long, and when she was awake she could play her heart out.

Muffin does not know much more about her family, except that they all would be proud of her. Muffin paid the ultimate sacrifice. She gave me her whole life so that I would be drawn closer to God.

My First Years with Muffin

In 1995, I was like a lot of people—I was working, searching, and striving for more. I wanted a better, faster car; more money; and fun. I put all that I could into investments and the stock market. I had a friend at work who worked as a probation officer also and we lived, ate, and slept thinking about the stock market. We were always looking for better returns and a bigger portfolio. Nothing was certain, yet all was invested, and we would lay everything on the line to get more.

We paid attention to brokers, read money magazines, and listened to every business report we could find. We never gave a thought to losing money. I had some bad returns, but I would only think about the good returns. It was the American dream: to have more and to want more. I was a slave to money; I was always taking a chance for bigger and better possessions. Spiritually, I thought I was all right. I prayed, and I went to church now and then. When I went to church, I always put something in the collection plate.

For several years, I would pray for a dog. I missed my little doggie, Mitsi, who had passed way from cancer. I was lucky to have had a dog almost all of my life—since I was five years old. This time, Mom had had enough; she did not want another dog. The responsibility of taking care of another dog was just too much. I had never really asked God for anything like a pet before. I always asked him to watch over my family and myself. I would ask God to help us in times of sickness and distress and to help us in times of need. I had never thought about asking him for something like a pet. During this time without Mitsi, I asked God to send me another dog … that was, whenever I thought to pray.

I thought about many breeds of dogs but I wanted a breed that I never had before. I decided to chose a bichon frise because I have talked to many people who owned one and all of them said the same thing: "It was the best dog I have ever owned." I have had many dogs over my life, and Muffin was truly the best dog I have ever owned.

It was not until I had written these words that I realized that God often has a better plan for us than we could ever realize. On a sunny afternoon in April 1995, I took a ride with my Mom to a pet store in Cherry Hill, New Jersey. My prayers were about to be answered. There she was, behind a glass case in a window display: the cutest little puppy I have ever seen. She was a bichon frise, a white powder puff, and she was all of six inches tall. I pressed my nose against the glass. I will never forget the first time I looked into those beautiful eyes. It was truly love at first sight. In that brief moment, our souls were united forever. As I was walking away, she was scratching the window with her left front paw as if to say, "Hey, where are you going?" She had me at her first stare.

It was like I robbed the store. I counted out the money and gave it to the cashier. I took her into my arms, and out the door we went. We made our way into the parking lot and then into the car. I thought it best for Mom and Muffin to sit in the backseat. That just seemed the safest way to travel with a new, tiny puppy.

We were not that far along when I looked into the rearview mirror. Muffin was stretching up with all that she had to reach my mom's chin, and was licking her over and over again. Muffin knew just how to win her over. She had already stolen my heart for life. It was only a matter of time before Mom would feel the same way about Muffin. Muffin was the first dog Mom truly loved. She had just tolerated the other dogs we'd had.

When we got home, we gave Muffin her first bath. She hated water, especially when she got her head wet. After a fast towel dry, Muffin would shake off, and she would be the happiest dog in the world. She would run from room to room, rubbing her body against the sofa and chairs, and she would finish with a rollover on her back, squirming and snorting along the way. I am not sure whether she was happy about being clean or just glad her bath was over.

Much to my surprise, family members had already chosen the name Macy for our dog. I stood firm on the name of Muffin, and I registered her with the American Kennel Club under the name of Muffin Bear. Whenever she was being scolded, we would use her chosen name followed with the question, "What did you do?"

Time passed quickly, and I spent many of my days with Muffin outside. I would take her for long walks through the neighborhood or to the dog park. We played for hours in the kitchen. She was not allowed anywhere else in the house because she could not get her training down to become housebroken.

Outside was Muffin's refuge; she could do no wrong there. Every time I went outside, she wanted to be out there with me. She would look out the back door and bark her head off as a puppy. She could see me through the back door and wanted out. I think that she had already formed a strong bond with us and always wanted to be with us, even at an early age.

When I would take Muffin out, she would stay outside forever and would seldom urinate. I would take her back into the kitchen, and to my annoyance, she would puddle on the floor. It was really frustrating. This went on for Muffin's entire first year. I yelled at her, scolded her, and rubbed her nose in it. Nothing worked.

One day when Muffin was urinating, I noticed a red stream of blood coming along with her urine. It turned out that all my talking, training, and working with her could not have helped her at all. Muffin had kidney stones that blocked her urinary tract. Once the stones moved out of the way, she could then urinate, which was usually in the house. She had absolutely no control over when she could go.

On September 27, 1996, Muffin was operated on; she had a cystotomy. The veterinarian cut her open and removed the stones. She needed surgery again on April 2, 1999, and yet again on October 5, 2000. After that date, we could give Muffin a newly developed food that prevented the stones from coming back. If it were not for the veterinarians of the Willingboro Clinic in New Jersey, Muffin would never have survived. Shortly after her first operation, she completed her training and would only go outside.

That first year was a learning experience for Muffin and me. One thing I realized is that you really have to talk to your dog. You need to talk to your dog all of the time to tell her what you are doing. That is how they learn to understand what you are saying.

This is also the way we should all be about praying. We should always be telling God what we are doing and asking him to lead us on the right path. Just like Muffin, God seldom talks to us, but he will guide us to the path that he wants us to pursue. We need to be strong to accept the path he is leading us down, even if it is not one we want to follow. If you choose not to follow his path, all other paths only lead to failure.

Muffin could not tell me that she was sick. I was clueless. I only knew what I wanted was not what she wanted. She probably wanted to be trained more than I wanted it for her. It is very easy to pick a path that we want to pursue and to ignore the path that God wants us to take. God always answers our prayers. Sometimes the answers come really quickly, and sometimes we have to search to find the right answer. I was only concerned about Muffin getting her training completed, thinking that she was disobedient. The harder path was to continue to work toward the goal with patience. The most amazing thing was that through all of this, Muffin still loved me with all of her heart, just as God loves us with all of his heart.

For me, this was a time of spiritual awakening. For the first time in a long time, I began to seek the Lord in my life. I began to listen more in church. I watched the television evangelists, and I began to pray more often. Muffin and I were thanking God for every day he had given us. She would often join me when I read the bible. I would read some scriptures out loud or say "Thank you Jesus for the day", and she would listen with her full attention as if she was getting every word I had spoken. I would say the verse over and over getting louder each time and her tail would wag even more. She would bark to join in. It was like she was saying, "Now you're getting it, God is hearing us".

We had it all. We had been blessed with a God who loved us, a loving family, and we had a wonderful home. We never went hungry. This is what mattered most in life, and it brought us our greatest joy.

In 1967, I accepted Jesus as my Lord and Savior. He has been in my heart ever since. There may have been times in my life when I had not been as close to Jesus as I am now, but he never left me. He has always been there and has forgiven my sins. Jesus gave his life to save us all from sin. His blood and sacrifice give us the promise of eternal life. This is the greatest gift that God has ever given us—His only begotten son. Jesus offers the forgiveness of sins and the way to salvation. He died on the cross to free us all from sin. From the moment the Holy Spirit enters our hearts we become changed forever. We need only to ask him into our hearts. There is no greater love than the love that Jesus has for all us. He is the Light of the World.

What Muffin Liked

One day, Muffin and I were walking along, and I told Muffin she was my puppy. She turned her head to look back at me as we continued along the way. She was delighted— her tail was wagging. From that day on, I told Muffin a million times that she was my puppy, especially when we would go to sleep at night. I would also tell her the story of how she left her mother, father, sisters, and brothers. She went on an airplane, was taken to a store, and in less than two hours, she was in my arms. She loved hearing her story. Sometimes I would sing her a little song while in bed. After that, we would be out like a light.

Muffin loved to eat. She would eat just about anything you gave her. As a puppy, she once tried to eat a flower. If I did not have a snack for the evening, Muffin would take her place across from me on the living room floor. She would stare at me as if to say, "Okay, what are we going to have tonight?" She loved cakes, candies, or anything that was sweet. Ice cream was her favorite, but she was never allowed to have it because of her kidney stones. She would do fine with pretzels or potato chips. She would eat a piece of sandwich, bread and all. She loved spaghetti sauce or any kind of soup over her dry food. Pizza was her favorite. Peanut butter would make her chew and chew. She loved to see me imitating her chewing right back at her. I would laugh, and she loved to see me happy. She would do her happy dance around the floor. She ate whatever I ate. I would always tell Muffin, "You get what I get." After a while, I would just say that and she knew that treat was coming. She would look into my hands to see what I had for her.

Muffin liked to see me kiss my mom, my girlfriend, Pat, or any of my relatives. She liked lying on my lap while I was stretched out on the sofa. She liked sleeping in bed at night or taking an afternoon nap. She would stay with me all the while. Even when I was sick, she would help me recover. She liked snuggling on long winter nights. She would crawl underneath the covers, and I would not see her until morning. She loved it when I talked to her, tilting her back and forth as if she understood every word I was saying. She loved hearing about my day, especially when no one else did.

She loved getting up in the morning and having some cereal, begging for breakfast and sausage until it was all gone. She would stare at me until I promised her more. Then I would tell her, "in your dish," and she would run to it as if I promised her the world.

She loved to go for walks. The mere sight of her leash sent her into a tizzy of loops and swirls until we made it to the sidewalk. I would always remind her never to go into the street. She was trained never to go into the street, even when she was off her leash, unless I allowed it. She had to be taught that because we lived on a very busy street. If she entered the roadway, she could be killed. Once in a great while, people walking their dogs would taunt Muffin. They would stand across the street looking at her, trying to entice her to cross the street. I would simply remind Muffin to stay and not to go into the street. She would stay and they would move along.

Muffin would often accompany me when I would garden. She loved to get up early and be my helper. She would find herself a shady spot, because she hated the heat. She would go under a tree or the car to stay cool. Then she would watch my every move.

One bright and beautiful day, I was working in the front yard and saw a young fellow who was parked at the curb, reading the paper. As I looked at him, I noticed him looking over the top of the paper. He was watching Muffin, and I think he was waiting for me to leave her alone. If I had left her there, I probably would never have seen her again. I took Muffin around back, and he immediately drove off. Muffin and I both liked the fact that nothing bad happened to her on that day.

On a cold winter night when Muffin was very young, she gave me the look. I was stretched out on the sofa, and going outside was the last thing I wanted to do. She had to go. She ran out the back door and kept going. It was snowing, and this was the first time she had ever seen snow. She ran three laps around the house. She then stopped and looked at me in utter amazement, as if nothing had happened. To say that she loved the snow is an understatement.

The snow brings back many memories for me. One by one, all my shoveling partners left me. My dad passed away from Alzheimer's disease in 1988. Both of my sisters got married and moved away. Mom is too old to shovel snow, but probably still would want to shovel if she could ... I won't dare let her. Muffin always liked to be with me in the snow. She would stay with me for hours while I shoveled. She was the most loyal helper God could ever have sent me.

Everyone knew Muffin. A school is located just down the street form our house. Over the years, the children learned to call Muffin by name, and they looked for her on their way home from school.

Muffy could be very protective with adults. She would never let anyone near the house or car. Yet, if I took her to see Dr. Lawrence Wolf, her veterinarian, she would allow him to do anything he had to, as long as I was in the room with her.

I worked on Muffin from the time she was a puppy. Saturday was her beauty day. I would brush her and check her to see that she was all right. She even allowed me to scrub her teeth every week. Dr. Wolf would have to show everyone her pearly whites during her vet visits. She had beautiful white teeth her entire life.

Muffin loved the holidays, especially Halloween. She would watch and wait for the children to come to our house. She would help me answer the door, sniffing her way almost outside. She loved looking out the front window and waiting for me to come home. She would stay there all day until I returned home. She loved Thanksgiving and having her portion of the turkey. At Christmas, she loved being there to watch us open our gifts and then opening her own.

Muffin loved to listen to Christian rock—the louder the better. She would lie down and watch while I danced or exercised. Even when I worked out, she would be there as my workout buddy. She loved waiting on Saturday mornings for my girlfriend, Pat, to come over.

One thing Muffin did not like was seeing me argue with my mom. She liked everyone to be happy all the time. She also hated fireworks. When she was very young, I took her along to watch fireworks at the river. I had to go to the bathroom. When I returned, Pat told me that Muffin had pulled herself free in the crowd. I scurried around the crowd and eventually found her with another couple. I guess she thought they would protect her while she was lost. Those were the worst ten minutes of my life.

Muffin did not like ambulances, either. My mom was in a car accident, and Muffin had been along for the ride. Mom had a concussion and had to be taken to the hospital in an ambulance. Muffin was left with a person close to the accident scene. When I found out, I went to the hospital and then went after Muffin. She was in a cage at a farm stand, scared to death and shaking when I found her. The farmer there had taken care of her after the accident. Muffin was glad to make it home, and I am glad I found her. Thank God Mom recovered from the concussion after an overnight stay in the hospital. From that day forward, Muffin hated car rides and ambulances.

In the year 2000, I became determined that I would no longer serve the world of investments. I systematically sold my shares in my various mutual funds. I wanted to put Christ first in my life and to try to serve him more than anything else. I never looked back. When you put your faith in God, you can sleep a lot better at night. Gambling all that I had just did not make sense anymore. Nothing should stand between God and us.

One day in 2004 while I was relaxing with Muffin, I realized how much Muffin loved me. I was thinking about her love. A revelation came to me that God loved me more than Muffin loved me. God spoke to my heart saying, "I love you more, my son." The tears came down like a heavy rain. That is how God's love led me closer to our Savior. Muffin's pure love for Mom and me was strong as steel. I realized that God's love is even greater. I knew he loved us, but until that day, I never truly fathomed how deep God's love is for all of us. This was a turning point in my life.

Mark 12:30 says that each of us should love the Lord with all our hearts, all our minds, all our souls, and all our strength. Muffin lived her life in that exact same way toward me. Her love was pure and unconditional. From that day when God spoke to me, I realized that I needed to strive to serve the Lord the way Muffin served me. Many people who own pets have experienced this kind of love. I wonder how many people have realized what I realized about God's deep and unconditional love. This is the reason God has called me to write this book: to allow me tell the story of his never-ending love for his children. Take a good look at your pet. You know how deep your pet's love is for you. I can honestly tell you that God loves you more.

When Muffin came into my life, it was no mistake. It was part of God's plan for my life. When you look at your pet, I hope you realize how much your pet loves you. He is giving up his life for you. It is wonderful to feel the purity of God's love and to realize that he has a plan for all of us, which, for some us, includes a pet that truly loves us.

If you open your heart to Jesus and your Bible, your life will be changed forever. Day by day, as you seek the Lord, your life will slowly change. Your actions and deeds will benefit others, as well as yourself. Your life will be filled with love and sharing with others. You will be living a life worthy of his plan. You will give more of what you own away to those who need it by helping those people less fortunate than yourself. Also, you will help those who are sick, poor, or down. When it comes time to meet Jesus, he will welcome you into his kingdom. He will love you for living a life worthy of walking heaven's streets of gold.

Accepting the Lord as your Savior is the first step. The hard part is to follow him. It is much easier and seems natural to do what we want to do. It is much harder to allow the Lord into our lives and follow him where he is directing us. If you do follow him day by day, you will be changed. You will become clay in God's hands. He will mold you into a beautiful person. Christ will live through you.

God will supply you with all your needs and answer your prayers. I once prayed about a friend I had lost contact with. She held a special place in my heart. I prayed to God that I would see her again to know that she was all right. It took a while, but he eventually answered my prayer. It turns out that she was just fine. God saw to it that we were reunited and that our friendship would always be there.

A Long Goodbye

In March 2009, I was in a bookstore with Pat. We were looking at a book about bichon frises. We saw a chart on their life expectancy and read that the bichon could live ten to fifteen years. Muffin was rapidly approaching fifteen years old. At first, I was sad to know this. Then I realized how truly lucky I was to have had Muffin for as long as I did. Realizing this, I was determined to enjoy every day with her even more. Each day we shared together was a blessing from God.

Muffin was such a part of our lives that we never really gave a thought to how long we had her. I prayed for God to watch over her, and he always did. Until that day in the bookstore, I had never realized that Muffin had exceeded her life expectancy. I knew she was getting older, but I just did not want to think about it.

Muffin slept a little bit more as she grew older, but she still was always with me. She would get up with me early in the morning to watch me garden or wash my car. She would find herself a special spot in the shade, and then all was right in her world. She always kept her eyes on me, those eyes that spoke to me, saying, "I love you with all of my heart."

In early May 2009, I noticed that Muffin had developed a cough. She would only cough one or tines per week and just for a few seconds. She would then go about her life as if nothing were wrong. By the middle of May, she was coughing every day and about once every two hours. I had an appointment on May 21, 2009, for her with Dr. Wolf. He is the most experienced veterinarian I know. I knew Muffin would need all the help she could get, as I had a bad feeling about this cough. Indeed, it was serious. Muffin was put on medicine to see how she would respond.

On June 6, 2009, Dr. Wolf had a follow-up appointment with Muffin. Muffin's X-ray showed she had pneumonia. Her medicine was not helping her, and her cough was getting worse. We took her back to the veterinarian on June 15, 2009. She was put on a special cough syrup that Dr. Wolf and a pharmacist formulated for her. This medicine helped her the most, but her cough still continued to worsen.

Under Dr. Wolf's direction, Muffin was taken to the specialist on June 19, 2009. Mom and I spent the day there, seeking treatment for Muffin. They found out Muffin had Cushing's disease, but that was considered minor. More importantly, she had a tumor in one lung and the makings of a second tumor in her other lung. Sadly, given her age and the developing second tumor, there was no going forward with further medical treatment other than what we were already doing. Surgery was not an option.

We continued loving Muffin more and more. We realized that our time with her was running out. We gave her medicine around the clock. I carried Muffin in my arms to take her outside in the middle of the night to make her comfortable. I also smashed up cough drops and allowed her to have them whenever she needed them.

I took Muffin outside all the time, since that was where she loved being the most. We went for little walks. Day by day I could see her getting a little weaker. On July 20, 2009, I worked eleven hours and did not arrive home until after 7:00 PM. I wondered if I would ever see Muffin again that night, and I was so happy I did. There was a new development now, however: Muffin had decided that she was no longer going to eat. She would only take some water. She did, however, eat some watermelon. She always loved that.

Muffin also started looking upward that night. It was as if she was looking up to heaven. She very rarely took her head down from that point on. This continued for two more days. She could hardly go to sleep.

On the night of July 22, 2009, I took Muffin to bed. No one got a sound night's sleep that night. I left the radio on, gently playing Christian music. Both of us felt better knowing that Jesus was with us. The music calmed our souls. I spent the night holding Muffin and crying. After all, whenever I was sick, she never left my side. It was the least I could do.

At 7:00 AM on July 23, 2009, I made the hardest call of my life. The most considerate female voice came on the line, and I scheduled a 9:00 AM appointment for Muffin. The assistant said she was very sorry Muffin had to be put down.

I never let Muffin out of my arms for the rest of our time together. I took her for a final walk. I carried her to the mailbox, putting her down at all the trees along the way. She loved finding the scents of other dogs. She looked back at me as if she knew this was our last time together. She loved having me hold her in my arms. We kissed each other.

When we got home, I sat her next to the back step on the grass. She lay there as I went into the house to bring her a treat. I put a dish of ice cream right in front of her. She got up and had the one thing she could never have. She licked and licked at her favorite treat but could not finish it all. It was the first food I had ever given her, and now it was the last.

Just about then, my neighbor, June Jacoby, came around the corner and saw the tears running down my face. I told her I was putting Muffin to sleep. She shared in my sorrow. The Jacobys are just like second parents to me. They have always showed by example how to love thy neighbor. To love thy neighbor is the second commandment. I have already explained God's greatest commandment of all, which is the central theme of Muffin's love: to serve God with all that you have. These verses can be found in Matthew 22:37–40 and are described as God's most important commandments.

Time seemed to have accelerated; it was our final ride. As I was walking toward the car, a busload of children was coming down the street. A young girl on the bus looked and saw me carrying Muffin to the car. She squealed in delight, yelling to her friends, "Look at that cute doggie!" Even on her final day, she still had the magic of attraction. She remains a puppy forever.

We reached the Willingboro Veterinary Clinic in no time. Dr. Wolf noticed us out in the lobby. He said, "I guess it's time." There was only one other person in the lobby: a young lady with her dog. As I was walked by, I uttered these words to her: "I want you to cherish every moment you have with your dog."

We entered the examination room. I placed Muffin on the table. I told Dr. Wolf about Muffin constantly looking up and that her tongue was turning black. We both thought this was maybe from a lack of oxygen. She was trying to keep her airway open.

Muffin did not look up once during that whole morning. The calm that came over Muffin was an answer to my prayers. That calmness also came over Mom and me as we entered the clinic. She had suffered so much, but the peace that only God can grant came over each of us. As I sat down in the chair, I placed my right hand under Muffin's face. Muffin and I were face-to-face, eye-to-eye. We never broke contact. I was petting her the whole time. I could see Dr. Wolf giving Muffin the iridescent pink fluid flowing out of the needle. She never closed her eyes that day. It was Muffin's final way to say to me that she would never leave me. Our souls are united forever. *I will never let you go*, I thought. I was still petting Muffin when they told me she was gone. I did not realize it because her eyes were still open. She looked as peaceful as ever. In twenty seconds, she entered eternity. That was the last time I looked into those eyes. I took my hand from under her head and reluctantly let go. We said goodbye. Muffin was left at the veterinarian's clinic to be cremated.

Next, an assistant came into the room. She made us a paw print of Muffin, and we had a conversation. I told her that Muffin had a pure heart and that Muffin was about love. I pray that someday I will again see those eyes and that little round face that I had just held in my hand. I pray that someday I will see my soul mate again.

There are very few moments in our lives when we can truly feel God's presence. From the moment that we entered the clinic, God was with us. It was the first time that Muffin did not get nervous when she was there. God's peace filled us all. God was there, and he never let go.

For the next several days, darkness filled our lives. Our hearts were filled with sorrow, realizing that we had lost our best friend. We cried and laughed, remembering the crazy things she did for us. We realized that Muffin's memory would be in our hearts forever.

Outside the Willingboro Veterinarian Clinic, there is a rock garden where people can leave a rock in memory of their pets. During the week, we painted a rock that reads,

"Muffin's love saved forever." There is a heart and a cross in each corner of the stone, signifying her love that led me to the cross. I remembered that day in 2004 when I realized how deep God's love is for all of us, and that Muffin was a wonderful part of God's plan for me.

One week later, there was a bad storm at home. The power went out throughout the neighborhood. I was returning home from work. People were milling about in the darkness. We had dinner by candlelight. I went to bed early. After I got into to bed, I looked over at my bichon frise calendar on the wall. There was a beautiful picture of a bichon. Moonlight was hitting in the exact spot where the picture was hanging. It was the only thing lit in the entire house, glowing from the moonlight. I called Mom in to see the picture. It was as if Muffin was continuing to watch over us, just as she did when we went to sleep at night. From out of the darkness, there came a glimmer of light and hope that Muffin was where she belonged.

Christmas of 2009 was missing something. For fourteen years, Muffin was always there to open the packages. Her collar now hangs where her Christmas stocking once did and her paw print is on display in the china closet. Her absence inspired me to want to complete Muffin's story more than ever.

Muffin's love led me to the realization of God's perfect love for us all. Muffin loved her family with all her heart, mind, soul, and strength. Each of us needs to try seek God just the way Muffin sought to love her family.

We all need to live the best lives we can. We need to open our hearts to Jesus so that he will guide us every step of the way. Seek him with all that you have. Our greatest challenge lies before us. There will come a day when we take our last breaths, just as Muffin did. If you have lived a life in faith and have come to the Father through Jesus

Christ, heaven is waiting for you. It will be the biggest, brightest experience that anyone could ever have. We will all be united with those who have become children of God. The lamb shall lie down with the lion, and I shall lie down with the dog I will always love: Muffin Bear. I cannot wait to look into her beautiful eyes again. Heaven is just a bark away.

My Life as a Probation Officer

Before I became a probation officer I asked God to send me to a job where I could best serve him and others. It took a few years but it finally happened. On March 26, 1985, I began my career as an investigator working in the juvenile section of the probation division writing restitution reports. It was my job to prepare the reports for the court when a juvenile committed theft. The report would be presented in court to help determine how much money was owed to the victims of crime.

I was promoted as a probation officer in 1987 and years later became a senior probation officer. Respectively I worked in the community service section and remained in adult criminal supervision for the rest of my career working caseloads involving all types of crime. The people I supervised were sex offenders, arsonists, wife beaters, drug addicts, and thieves. Their occupations were a minister, cooks, waitresses, truck drivers, landscapers and just about any other job you can think of that is out there in the world. They were mothers, fathers, sisters and brothers. They were people that made mistakes. The most important thing for an officer is to see that the probationers obey their conditions of probation. That means obeying the law, working, and paying on their fines. My job was to show them their way. If they did not comply I would take them back to court.

During my first ten years as a probation officer I was tough as nails as I hammered the probationers into compliance. Some people came into compliance and the ones that did not ended up in prison. During that time I was more concerned about what I wanted not what others wanted or needed. I worked with my fellow officers but it was more like a competition. We were taught as officers to be in control of the probationers and to be aggressive in getting our job done.

Being Humble

In 1995, coincidentally the year I got Muffin I decided to try another approach with my people on probation, a new way of supervision had begun. I was secure enough in my job to become a better helper. God helped me find a verse in the Bible that I just had to implement.

Philippians: 2- 3-5 Don't be selfish; don't try to impress others. Be humble, thinking of others as better than yourselves. Do not look out only for your own interest, but take an interest in others.

You must have the same attitude that Jesus Christ had.

This became my guiding principal to become a better probation officer. I began to accept others with all the flaws they brought along with them by being non-judgmental. I listened to others to better understand their life circumstances. We all need to be more concerned about the people we work with including our coworkers rather than ourselves, in doing so we become more Christ-like.

People know when you care about them, they can see it in your actions and the way you express yourself. When they seek help through you they will benefit and you will benefit.

In 2004, when I realized how much God loved me, things really began to change. I remember one year that not one person was sent to prison. I worked on cases helping people overcome anger, drug addictions, and issues with stealing. I helped more people in my first year with this new approach then I did in my first ten years as a probation officer.

I worked under supervisors that gave me absolute control over the people I supervised. We signed petitions of the court that allowed some of the probationers to be taken off of probation early because of their exceptional compliance. The people who were not in compliance were brought back to court with the main objective geared towards self-betterment. Probationers were given more time to come into compliance and most did not have to go to jail. I helped people every way I could including my coworkers. I had the respect of nearly everyone I worked with.

For 25 years, I was a probation officer and had the blessing of meeting hundreds of people. My goal as an officer was to point my people in the right direction and do anything to help them change their lives for the better. Often I would ask them about going to church, and reading the Bible.

It was best when I had the opportunity to point them in the direction of the cross. I felt the presence of God in their lives, and my own life. I saw the changes Jesus made. There was nothing better than to bear witness to God's blessings in their lives.

During my career as a probation officer I received customer service awards in 2008 and 2009. I received these awards because someone outside the probation division had nominated me for these awards. In July 2009 the month and year Muffin went to heaven God lifted me up with recognition by blessing me with the Meritorious Service

Award. Very few officers are given this honor. I was honored for outstanding service above and beyond the call of duty. By being humble I was I was recognized for helping others, and accomplishing great works.

On July 1, 2010 I retired from the probation division to begin a new phase in my life. During the month I was honored with two retirement dinners. I felt the love we shared in the common bond of our vocation. We have mutual respect for everyone and I have gained many life long friends that I will always keep in touch with.

I spent my entire life guiding people to doing the right thing, and it was time for me to the right thing. It was not planned, but I prayed and retiring was the course that God showed me. Right now I am needed at home and that is where I will be. I really do believe that a part of this was God leading me to finish writing *Muffin's Love*. I will continue to follow God where ever he leads me.

The Presence of God

In 2005, while I was interviewing a probationer I realized that he was heavy into drugs, and I became nervous because I did not know where to place the probationer to help him with his addiction. As I was interviewing him I was praying to God to help this man. I was multi-tasking. The probationer did not know that I was praying. As I was praying I could feel my nerves settling down, and Jesus coming in. God helped me from that moment on to help this man. We both felt God's presence in the room that night. I found him a hospital where he could get detoxification free of charge. From then on he knew that I would always be there to help him. He had never been shown such compassion. His exposure with law enforcement had always been very negative. He had already done time in a state prison for many years. He thought I was just another officer looking to put him away. I continued to work with him through out his life and we became friends. It was wonderful to see the changes God made in his life. Needless to say he never returned to jail again. He kept in touch with me even after he was off of probation. We both realized that God was with us that night when we needed him the most and he never let us go.

Pray Daily

People have asked me how I survived in such a demanding job. The secret to my success is that every day should always start with a prayer. About five minutes out on my drive into work I would pass by a church with two red doors that had a white cross on each door. There as I would pass by I would thank God for another day. I would reach out my hand and ask God to watch over everyone and Muffin. Sometimes I would ask God to help me with all that I was about to encounter at work. Sometimes I would ask God to keep me from turning the car around. Thank God I never turned around. Being a probation officer was a demanding job. All jobs these days are demanding. Worse yet you might be looking for a job. No matter what our situation in life we all need to pray daily to ask God to help us in our challenges.

A client I had worked with for five years became one of the most important clients that I have ever supervised. He asked me to attend his graduation ceremony from a drug program. I was honored to attend and realized that most of the other people graduating that night had family members there to enjoy in their success. That is when it dawned on me that I was his only family and just how much he cared for me. Working together we made an impact on his life.

During his probationary term he always kept all of his office appointments. Gradually over time I could see that he was becoming ill with a persistent cough which later was diagnosed as lung cancer. I told him that he no longer had to report for his office appointment to see me and could just call in to tell me how he was doing. He insisted on coming to see me. On our last visit together we talked about him being sick and he could easily go back to his old way of life but he would not allow that because of the new way of life he had found through Jesus. We also talked about what heaven would be like, and that we will look for each other in eternity. It was the most important conversation I have ever had with someone on probation.

To close a case of a probationer an officer must have proof that his client has died. One year later his sister finally sent me a prayer card to close the case in his behalf. I was amazed to find out that he attended the church of the two red doors where I would pray every day for God to watch over my family and Muffin as I drove by. His prayer card showed that he had dedicated his life to the Lord. I had joined him through prayer many times without even knowing it .God knew and he showed me how important that church was to the both of us.

Daily Growth

I hope that I have given you an idea of what it is like to be a probation officer but more importantly how God helps us grow day by day. A little bit every day we become stronger, and wiser. Slowly we are brought up in tiny increments. It is almost like we do not even realize the changes that have taken place. Then when we look back at our lives we are in wonder of the amazing journey that we are on, and could not even imagine what it would be like without Jesus in our lives. I may not be rich in this world but I know that I am worth a fortune in heaven. I want to stay under God's grace to enjoy the gifts he has given me and the gifts he has promised me.

I know that by reading and following *Muffin's Love* teachings you will be blessed. I want you to give your pet a hug from me. Think about how your life has changed since you owned your best friend. You will be absolutely fascinated at what you will find. There was a wonderful transformation in my life that went on for fourteen years with Muffin. You may actually realize the spiritual growth that has taken place the longer you have had your pet if you take the time to look for it. God sent us a best friend in Muffin all because I asked him in prayer to send me a dog. He sent me a teacher who listened and loved me with all of her heart. God let his light shine upon us and I am blessed.

The Face of Love

After a stressful day I would often use a relaxation technique that helped me settle down. At first I would stare at Muffin's face, but over time I thought of a better face. It has to be the one soul that you know is pure, unfailing, one of the few constants in your life. Ultimately it should be the face of Jesus. Some one who will always be there deep within your heart. He is a part of you that will never leave you. You know that he loves you and that he gave his life for you. It does not matter where you are you just think about the face of love.

With your eyes closed think only of the face of love. It does not matter where you are physically as long as mentally you are relaxing thinking of the face of love. Breath deep breaths inhaling through your nose and exhaling through your mouth. Relaxing with every breath you take, deeper and deeper into relaxation. If you fall asleep that is alright. I promise you inevitably someone will wake you up. After about ten minutes of relaxing this way you will feel better. By using this technique over and over again the behavior will reduce your stress level so that eventually you can relax just by thinking of the face of love when ever you need to calm down.

If you know that you are going to be or are in a stressful situation think of the face of Jesus. You know that he will never leave you. Think of him every day. If you are having a really bad day- think of him every hour. Just thinking of Jesus will help you calm down. He is with every breath you take.

The Journey of Life

There is not a day that goes by that I do not think of Muffin. Her life has had a profound effect on our family. Her love has made me think endlessly about God's love. Since she has moved on I have read about love in the Bible to reach a better understanding of the greatest human emotion God has ever given us.

What I realized is that when we look at ourselves in the mirror we must learn to accept the person we see in the mirror. You can not want to be someone else. You have to accept yourself for the person you are before you can accomplish anything in life. Every night when I came home from work Muffin would be in the front window looking for me to arrive. Sometimes Mom would remind her to wait for me but most of the time she would be on guard for my arrival. When I came in she would run into the room and wait for me to acknowledge her. When I did she would run from room to room waging her tail, and barking her head off. Muffin helped me to accept the person I am and to love my family. When I saw her happiness I realized that it was a blessing to be home where it is safe and sound. Also that

God created us with the miracle of life and he gives us his wondrous love.

1 Corinthians 13:30- " There are three things that will last forever: Faith, hope and love. The greatest of these is love." We have to have faith in ourselves before we can have faith in others. I believe deep down in my soul that Muffin will never leave me. She has not left me for over a year now and I know that she never will. She is in my heart forever. I have the hope of seeing Muffin again in eternity. Muffin's love will remain forever. I agree with every fiber of my being that love is the greatest human emotion.

Our life begins when God gives us our first breath. From that moment on we look for love in our lives. Without love our lives would not be worth living. As far back as I can remember I can still feel the love that my Mom gives me. I remember being in a room of complete strangers. They were all pointing to a small round opening saying, "Look into that window". The nurses were showing me that my Mom was right there in the window waving and smiling. I was three years old and was about to have my tonsils out but that did not matter because Mom was there. The mere sight of her brought the feeling of her love and security. I can still feel that love today.

The next vivid memory I have was a Sunday walk from church with Mom, Dad, and my sisters Jennifer and Lydia. We were all dressed up walking hand in hand. I had a picture that I drew of Jesus that someone helped me write God is love. We walked along the sidewalk under the shade of the trees with a gentle breeze blowing on a wonderful spring day. I was holding my Daddy's hand, and the world did not seem as huge as it does when you are four years old. The love that was there that day still burns brightly in my heart.

As a young man I served as a president of a youth organization. There I learned about brotherly love. We helped one another in times of need, and the community by supporting local charities. During this time I learned to give to the church and others by loving thy neighbor.

If we are fortunate we have many family members when we start our lives. As time goes on we grow older and one by one we lose the ones we love. My Father, Grand Parents and most of my Aunts and Uncles have all gone on. I believe that many of them are waiting for me in heaven. When we are young we have the love of our God and family given to us but as we become adults we must find most our love through our faith in God.

The world is full of choices. It would be easy to want the ways of the world. Some might not even concern themselves with the path of righteousness. They are perfectly fine with wanting all the world has to offer. Some may not even give a thought about what they are giving up. They may not make it into heaven, and there will be no treasures found there. The wages of sin is death. To be reunited with my love ones in heaven is everything to me.

The greatest teacher of all is God. The only choice that we do not have to make is when God created us. From the time we begin to grow the choices become our own. If we choose the Way our lives will be filled with love. My Daddy's hand left mine but God's hand is always there to guide me along the journey of life. When I start to slip I can always feel his strong hand to help lead me on to the narrow path to heaven. I hope that you will make the right choices in life so that you will feel the power of God's love.

Love is truly the greatest of human emotions that will last forever, included in that love is our family and our neighbors whose bonds will never be broken. They are our treasures here on earth and in heaven. Muffin is included in this love.

There is a place deep within our hearts were love flows. It is that warm feeling we experience inside when we look at the ocean, hear a song, read a verse, or hold the hand of someone. Muffin takes me to the place that brought out the emotions of my journey of life so far, that place in your heart where love is found. That feeling we experience is love. This is the place in your heart where God is at and eternity can be found there. Love will last forever, and God is love.

Muffin Tells Her Story

I thought it might be nice to write a children's version of *Muffin's Love* to be read to them, but you might like this version of the story also.

God created the heavens and the earth with everything in it. God is truly awesome. On a quiet dark night Muffin was created by God. He took the time to create my special doggie. I hope that someday he will create you a special doggie.

Here is what Muffin said, "Well Hello God! Thank you for giving me my life. I promise that I will always be a good doggie and that I will love and serve my master. I will always listen to him and try to obey him.

My Mom is beautiful. I hope that I will grow up to look just like her. She is white and fluffy all over. Her fur reminds me of the snow. I want to look just like her when I grow up. I am a Bichon. Mom sure feels good to snuggle up with and she keeps me warm at night. She always makes sure that I am never hungry. She gives me everything I need, but most of all she gives me love.

I remember when I lived together with my family. We all stayed together. I saw Mom and Dad every day. I would play all I wanted with my brothers, and sisters. We had so much fun together that I will never forget them. I will always be thankful for the endless days I spent with my family.

My Mom and Dad told me that one day I would leave them to be with my master. I always wondered who that might be. They told me that told me it would be a man who asked God for a dog, and that I was going to be a special dog. Well when I heard that I was going to be a special doggie I ran around in circles from being so happy. Then something amazing happened. A noise from deep down inside of me suddenly came out. It was my first bark. I barked a huge bark to tell my family I was a special doggie.

It wasn't long after that day that a nice man came and put me in a little cage. They placed me in an airplane in a space all by myself but I was not afraid because I was doing what God, and my parents told me to do. That is what we call faith.

The next thing I knew I was looking out into one of the biggest stores I have ever seen. Come to think of it, it was the only store I have ever seen. No one came for hours even to look at me. Hey wait a minute there was someone over there. I wondered what I could do so that man would see me ? I know, I'll go right in front of the glass so he has to see me. Well he came right over and looked right into my eyes and I felt very warm all over. I felt love just like when I looked at Mom. The man started walking away so the only thing I could do was to scratch on the glass to get his attention. He walked away anyway and I felt really sad in my heart. I continued to watch him and noticed he was giving the store owner something but I was so far away I did not know what it was. The next thing I knew I was out of the case and in the arms of the man I loved. I hoped I never have to leave this man ever again. Wishes do come true.

Muffin's Love

From that day on I went home to live with my master Frank and his Mom. God had created me to be with Frank just like my parents knew what was going to happen. Frank's prayer was answered. They named me Muffin Bear. I learned how to bark to go outside when I had to go to the bathroom. I was taught never to go into the street unless an adult was with me, also to stay away from strangers. We went for walks together, ate good food together, and played together. We loved the fresh air outside and exercising. Frank and his Mom would give me baths and scrubbed my teeth. I loved feeling clean, but you know I am a doggie so I loved getting dirty. I loved playing in the snow and digging holes in the dirt.

Often I would lye beside Frank while he read the Bible. Sometimes I would bark out a few verses myself, but Frank would just look at me and laugh. I guess only my doggie family could understand me. Before we would go to sleep at night we would say our prayers. We would thank Jesus for the day. Frank would tell me the story of how I came to live with him or sing me song to fall asleep by. Every day was a blessing.

Frank told me to love God with all our hearts so that we would receive the gift of salvation. That means Jesus gave his life so that we could go to heaven through the gift he has given us. I lived a long and happy life with Frank. I kept my promise to God to love and serve my family. Someday I will be with Frank in heaven. Thank you God for the life you have given us, but most important for the love you give us all. I am a special doggie. RRRRuuuFFF!"

The Gift

A long time ago on a deep dark night there was a glimmer of light that traveled across the Universe that grew brighter as the night went on to tell the world that Jesus Christ Our Savior was born. That light grew brighter, and continued to grow with Jesus.

Jesus began to walk his walk and talk his talk. He lived a life that only Jesus could. He was perfect in every way. He touched the lives of everyone he met. He shared his knowledge, compassion, and miracles with everyone he encountered along the way. His love was witnessed by all.

He gave all he could, and eventually he gave his life at Calvary to give us the promise of everlasting life. Today his light still shines brightly throughout the world. All you have to do is to let that light come into your heart, and in that moment your life will be changed forever. You will begin your journey with Jesus Christ.

At Christmas we give thanks to God for that first night when God gave us the greatest gift the world has ever known, and the promise that was given that night. His light will shine forever.

You are probably wondering why I included this Christmas passage in our story. It was written in 2008, the last Christmas I shared with Muffin. I believe God was showing me that I could write something worthy to give to others. He planted a seed in me that began to grow until the first words were written for *Muffin's Love* on August 1, 2009.

I wanted to get you into a Christmas mood. Maybe you are lucky enough to be eight years old with your Mom or Dad reading this to you. If not I want you to remember what it felt like to be eight years old again to remember when your parents asked if you were good and Santa Claus was going to bring you a present. If you were good you were golden. If you were bad and you admitted it you were probably fine as well. It is a great feeling knowing that you are going to receive a gift for doing the right thing. If you do the right thing with God you will receive the gifts of his blessings.

During the time Muffin and I were together we learned many important lessons. We learned how to: love and serve God, to love and serve others, to be humble and to enjoy the things that God gives us. We do not need the best of material possessions. We value our family and friendships the most. We find our joy in simple things like: just being together, reading the Bible, or a good book, having a cup of coffee, and waking up to be alive to see another day. We look back and see the love God has given us through his presence and through our family. We learned to pray more often to thank God for all he has given us, and to help us in our times of need. We should all try to live life this way. Ultimately God will pave the way to heaven.

If heaven is just a bark away you will receive the greatest gift of eternal life by joining Jesus and God in heaven. Eternal life compared to our earthly life is ten times ten times ten and beyond. In heaven we will be children of God made new again. When I get there I will kneel before Jesus and tears will fall. I probably will not even be able to get the words out of my mouth to thank him for all that he has given us. Our treasures in heaven will then be received. I believe that for some of us those treasures may include pets like Muffin.

I have given you all that I can. Suddenly it feels like I am eight years old again, knowing that I have striven to be good in the sight of God waiting for the best gift ever when you receive our story. Every day with Jesus should feel like Christmas. It feels like Christmas to me.

Test of Faith

I always felt that someday I would write a book. When Muffin went to heaven, I knew I had to share her story. To prepare her manuscript, I resurrected my 1995 computer, but I needed a printer. I was in a parking lot, ready to go into the store to buy one and a feeling came over me that I should call a computer company about printers. After seeing the prices, I made the call. A man told me to come to his company, and he would give me a printer. Thank you, Jesus, for leading me to a man with a good heart.

I prayed to God about how to launch *Muffin's Love*. The answer was found through CrossBooks. The evolution of this book has been a series of challenges. My hardest challenge is before me: to see this book become a reality. To have readers who want to experience Muffin's story will truly be a blessing. It is time for Muffin to go out into the world; she loves it out there. Dogs are mainstream because people love their pets. It is Muffin's new mission to bring Jesus into the mainstream, one reader at a time. When this book is in your hands, you will know I went forward with faith in God and that my dream came true through Jesus Christ.

I hope you learned from Muffin. I know I sure did. I sincerely hope you will be saved, read your Bible, pray daily, and listen to what God is telling you through your heart. The hard part is having the faith to do what he tells you to do. If he tells you to write a book, sing a song, or just talk to someone about Jesus, do it. God will show you the path to follow. You will be blessed. I hope that someday I will write again.

CPSIA information can be obtained at www.ICGtesting.com
Printed in the USA
BVOW011300290911

272351BV00001B/30/P